Chinese Quick Guides

POPULAR CHINESE PHRASES
AND EXPRESSIONS

Cathy Xiaoxia Zhou

LONG RIVER PRESS
San Francisco

Author: Cathy Xiaoxia Zhou
Editor: Lily Lijuan Zhou
Executive Editor: Eric Lock & John Parker
Designer: SinoMedia Ltd.
Illustrator: Wang Guofeng
Publishers: Zhang Ruizhi & Xu Mingqiang

First Edition   September 2004

ISBN 1-59265-027-9

Published in the United States of America by
Long River Press
3450 3rd ST., #4B, San Francisco, CA 94124
www.longriverpress.com
in association with Haiwen Audio-Video Publisher

Printed in China

Introduction

Popular Chinese Phrases and Expressions is designed to help foreign visitors, businesspeople and others who have learned some Chinese and want to socialize with the Chinese-speaking community.

Chinese words and expressions have a long history and deep cultural implications. Knowing the appropriate expressions for specific social occasions will demonstrate a great deal of respect for Chinese culture and help build strong friendships.

The phrases in this book are arranged according to the functions and situations in which they are used. They have been chosen because of the high frequency of their usage.

Contents

好运连连(hǎo yùn lián lián) May luck always accompany you.

新婚祝福 Marriage Blessings

新婚快乐(xīn hūn kuài lè) Best wishes for a happy marriage.

早生贵子(zǎo shēng guì zǐ) May you soon have a son.

白头偕老(bái tóu xié lǎo) May you live together to a ripe old age.

百年好合(bǎi nián hǎo hé) May your marriage last a hundred years.

花好月圆(huā hǎo yuè yuán) May your marriage be like beautiful flowers and a round moon.

永结同心(yǒng jié tóng xīn) Together forever.

团圆祈祷 Reunion Blessings

合家团圆(hé jiā tuán yuán) Here's to a happy family reunion.

欢聚一堂(huān jù yì táng) Here's to a happy reunion!

事业祝福 Business Blessings 38

马到成功 (mǎ dào chéng gōng) May you enjoy immediate success.

开业大吉 (kāi yè dà jí) May your business have an auspicious beginning.

一帆风顺 (yì fān fēng shùn) May the wind always be at your back.

事业有成 (shì yè yǒu chéng) May you have a rewarding career.

事业腾达 (shì yè téng dá) May your business be prosperous.

前程万里 (qián chéng wàn lǐ) May you have a promising future.

生意兴隆 (shēng yi xīng lóng) May your business flourish.

财源广进 (cái yuán guǎng jìn) May wealth be yours.

财运亨通 (cái yùn hēng tōng) Here's to good luck in money matters.

生日祝福 Birthday Wishes 56

生日快乐 (shēng rì kuài lè) Happy birthday.

长命百岁〔cháng mìng bǎi suì〕May you live to be a hundred.

见面问候 Greetings 60

幸会幸会〔xìng huì xìng huì〕It is a pleasure to meet you.

久仰久仰〔jiǔ yǎng jiǔ yǎng〕Glad to meet you.

久闻大名〔jiǔ wén dà míng〕I've heard many good things about you.

别来无恙〔bié lái wú yàng〕How have you been since we last met?

劝告 Advice 68

好自为之〔hǎo zì wéi zhī〕Conduct yourself well and make the best of it.

悬崖勒马〔xuán yá lè mǎ〕Pull back before it is too late.

回头是岸〔huí tóu shì àn〕Repent and salvation is at hand.

隔墙有耳〔gé qiáng yǒu ěr〕Walls have ears.

三思后行〔sān sī hòu xíng〕Look before you leap.

安慰 Consolation / Comfort 78

早日康复 (zǎo rì kāng fù) Get well soon.

好事多磨 (hǎo shì duō mó) Good things never come easily.

塞翁失马 (sài wēng shī mǎ) A loss may spell a gain.

东山再起 (dōng shān zài qǐ) Stage a comeback.

来日方长 (lái rì fāng cháng) There is ample time ahead of you/ There will be other opportunities.

破财消灾 (pò cái xiāo zāi) Such a loss may turn out to be a blessing.

岁岁 (碎碎) 平安 (suì suì píng ān) Peace every year.

节哀顺变 (jié āi shùn biàn) Don't be so sorrowful.

感谢 Gratitude 94

非常感谢 (fēi cháng gǎn xiè) Thank you very much.

感激不尽 (gǎn jī bú jìn) I am deeply indebted to you.

承蒙关照 (chéng méng guān zhào) Thank you for your care and consideration.

雪中送炭 (xuě zhōng sòng tàn) Thank you for your timely assistance.

道歉 Apology 102

对不起（duì bu qǐ）I'm sorry/Excuse me.

多多包涵（duō duō bāo hán）Please excuse (me for) what I have said/done.

自谦 Self-effacement 106

哪里哪里（nǎ li nǎ li）You are too kind. (Not at all).

马马虎虎（mǎ mǎ hū hū）It is just so-so.

班门弄斧（bān mén nòng fǔ）Display one's inadequate skills in front of an expert.

抛砖引玉（pāo zhuān yǐn yù）May my crude remarks draw forth others by abler men.

雕虫小技（diāo chóng xiǎo jì）It is an insignificant skill/It is nothing accomplished to speak of.

送别 Farewell 116

一路平安（yí lù píng ān）Bon voyage.

一路保重（yí lù bǎo zhòng）Take care on your journey.

一路顺风（yí lù shùn fēng）Have a pleasant journey. Bon

voyage.

慢走（màn zǒu）Take care.

走好（zǒu hǎo）Take care.

Top 10 Expressions

1. 幸会幸会 (xìng huì xìng huì)

   It is a pleasure to meet you. Page 61

2. 一路保重 (yí lù bǎo zhòng)

   Take care on your journey. Page 119

3. 哪里哪里 (nǎ li nǎ li) Not at all (thank you). Page 107

4. 多多包涵 (duō duō bāo hán)

   Please excuse (me for) what I have said/done. Page 105

5. 恭喜发财 (gōng xǐ fā cái) Wishing you good fortune. Page 7

6. 万事如意 (wàn shì rú yì)

   May everything go as you wish. Page 9

7. 新婚快乐 (xīn hūn kuài lè)

   Best wishes for a happy marriage. Page 23

8. 生日快乐 (shēng rì kuài lè) Happy birthday. Page 57

9. 早日康复 (zǎo rì kāng fù) Get well soon. Page 79

10. 合作愉快 (hé zuò yú kuài)

    May we have a fruitful cooperation. Page137

节日快乐

节日 (**jié rì**) means "holiday";
快乐 (**kuài lè**) "happy and merry".

节 日 快 乐

jié   rì   kuài   lè

Happy holiday!

This phrase is very frequently used when Chinese extend good wishes to friends and colleagues on any holiday, such as New Year's Day, Spring Festival, Lantern Festival, Labor Day, and the Mid-Autumn Festival.

3

给您拜年

给 (**gěi**) means "to give"; 您 (**nín**) "you"; 拜 (**bài**) literally "to kowtow"; 年 (**nián**) "year".

给 您 拜 年

gěi nín bài nián

Happy New Year!

From the first day of the new year (Spring Festival) to the fifteenth day (Lantern Festival) in the Chinese lunar calendar, Chinese greet each other using this expression with both hands folded in front of their chests when they first meet.

恭喜发财

恭喜 (**gōng xǐ**) means "congratulate";
发财 (**fā cái**) "make a fortune".

恭 喜 发 财

gōng xǐ fā cái

Wishing you good fortune.

Also used to welcome friends and colleagues during the Lunar New Year period.

万事如意

万事 (wàn shì) literally means "ten thousand things".
To Chinese 万事 suggests "a countless number of things";
如意 (rú yì) "according to (your) wish".

万 事 如 意

wàn shì rú yì

May everything go as you wish.

Used during the Lunar New Year and on other
occasions to wish people good fortune.

合家欢乐

合家 (hé jiā) means "the whole family";
欢乐 (huān lè) has the same meaning as 快乐 (kuài lè) "happy and merry".

合家欢乐

hé jiā huān lè

May your whole family enjoy happiness.

Used during the Lunar New Year and on other occasions to celebrate family gatherings.

11

心想事成

心想 (**xīn xiǎng**) means "thinking in heart";
事成 (**shì chéng**) "things to succeed/accomplish".

xīn xiǎng shì chéng

May all your wishes come true.

A personal greeting wishing people success in all their affairs.

13

工作顺利

工作 (**gōng zuò**) means "work or job";
顺利 (**shùn lì**) "smooth".

工作顺利

gōng zuò shùn lì

May your work go smoothly!

A wish to friends and business associates.

学习进步

学习 (**xué xí**) means "studies";
进步 (**jìn bù**) "progress".

学 习 进 步

xué xí jìn bù

Wishing you progress in your studies!

Used to wish students success in their studies.

17

步步高升

步 (bù) means "a step"; 步步 (bù bù) is doubled for emphasis;
高升 (gāo shēng) "to promote, to produce high".

步步高升

bù bù gāo shēng

May your career progress step by step.

Used to congratulate someone who has just
been promoted.

19

好运连连

好运 (hǎo yùn) means "good luck";
连连 (lián lián) "continually, in succession".

hǎo yùn lián lián

May luck always accompany you.

Used to wish someone continued good luck.

新婚快乐

新婚 (xīn hūn) means "newly married";
快乐 (kuài lè) "happy and merry" as we learned in
"新年快乐" (Happy New Year).

xīn hūn kuài lè

Best wishes for a happy marriage.

Used to congratulate newlyweds either at a
wedding party or elsewhere.

早生贵子

早生 (**zǎo shēng**) means "to produce soon";
贵子 (**guì zǐ**) "noble son".

早生贵子

zǎo shēng guì zǐ

May you soon have a son.

Used to congratulate newlyweds.

白头偕老

白头 (**bái tóu**) means literally "white hair";
偕老 (**xié lǎo**) "to accompany to a ripe old age".

白头偕老

bái tóu xié lǎo

May you live together to a ripe old age.

Used to congratulate newlyweds, wishing them a long life together.

百年好合

百年 (bǎi nián) means "a hundred years";
好合 (hǎo hé) "to join/connect so well".

百年好合

bǎi nián hǎo hé

May your marriage last a hundred years.

Used to congratulate the newly weds at wedding parties or on wedding cards.

花好月圆

花好 (huā hǎo) means "beautiful flowers";
月圆 (yuè yuán) "the round moon". To Chinese, round
moon has the connotation of perfection.

huā hǎo yuè yuán

May your marriage be like beautiful flowers and a round moon. (Harmonious)

Used to congratulate the newlyweds at wedding parties or on wedding cards.

31

永结同心

永结 (yǒng jié) means "to tie together forever";
同心 (tóng xīn) "united at heart".

永结同心

yǒng jié tóng xīn

Together forever.

Used to congratulate the newlyweds at wedding parties or on wedding cards.

合家团圆

合家 (hé jiā) means "the whole family";
团圆 (tuán yuán) "to get together".

hé jiā tuán yuán

Here's to a happy family reunion!

An often used wish, can be used as a toast at a family reunion party.

欢聚一堂

欢聚 (huān jù) means "to gather merrily";
一堂 (yì táng) "the same hall".

欢 聚 一 堂

huān jù yì táng

Here's to a happy reunion!

Used at any getting-together party, such as parties for alumni/alumnae or colleagues. This expression is more suitable for formal occasions.

马到成功

马到 (**mǎ dào**) means literally "upon arrival";
成功 (**chéng gōng**) "succeed/success".

马到成功

mǎ dào chéng gōng

May you enjoy immediate success.

A frequently used expression to describe quick and smooth success.

开业大吉

开业 (kāi yè) means "open for a business";
大吉 (dà jí) "auspicious".

开业大吉

kāi yè dà jí

May your business have an auspicious beginning.

Used on the first day of the commencement of a new business.

一帆风顺

一帆 (yì fān) means "sailing along";
风顺 (fēng shùn) "favorable wind".

一帆风顺

yì fān fēng shùn

May the wind always be at your back.

Used to express good wishes on any occasion, especially to somebody starting a new business or a new career.

事业有成

事业 (shì yè) means "career/occupation";
有成 (yǒu chéng) "have a success".

shì yè yǒu chéng

May you have a rewarding career.

Used to address somebody just starting a career or to congratulate somebody who has succeeded in his/her career.

事业腾达

事业 (shì yè) means "business or career";
腾达 (téng dá) "rising up".

事 业 腾 达

shì yè téng dá

May your business be prosperous!

Used to express good wishes for a successful business or career.

前程万里

前程 (qián chéng) means "future";
万里 (wàn lǐ) literally means "ten thousand miles".

前程万里

qián chéng wàn lǐ

May you have a promising future.

Used to express good wishes for a successful business or career.

生意兴隆

生意 (**shēng yì**) means "business";
兴隆 (**xīng lóng**) "prosperous and flourishing".

shēng yi xīng lóng

May your business flourish.

Used when a business is just opened, or as a
greeting on New Year's Day.

财源广进

财源 (**cái yuán**) means "source of fortune/wealth";
广进 (**guǎng jìn**) "come in grandly".

财源广进

cái yuán guǎng jìn

May wealth be yours.

Used when a business is just opened, or as a greeting on New Year's Day.

财运亨通

财运 (**cái yùn**) means "luck in moneymaking";
亨通 (**hēng tōng**) "prosper".

财运亨通

cái yùn hēng tōng

Here's to good luck in money matters.

Used when a business is just opened, or as a greeting on New Year's Day.

生日快乐

生日 (shēng rì) means "birthday";
快乐 (kuài lè) "happy and merry".

生日快乐

shēng rì kuài lè

Happy birthday.

The most frequently used expression for wishing somebody a happy birthday.

长命百岁

长命 (cháng mìng) means "long life";
百岁 (bǎi suì) "hundred years".

长命百岁

cháng mìng bǎi suì

May you live to be a hundred.

Frequently used expression for wishing somebody a happy birthday. Mostly to elderly person.

幸会幸会

幸 (**xìng**) means "lucky";
会 (**huì**) "to meet".

幸会幸会

xìng huì xìng huì

It is a pleasure to meet you.

This expression can serve as a response when you are introduced to somebody or to a group of persons.

久仰久仰

久 (**jiǔ**) means "long time";
仰 (**yǎng**) "admire/respect".

久仰久仰

jiǔ yǎng jiǔ yǎng

Glad to meet you.

This expression is used as a courteous response when somebody introduces his/her name to you. It implies his/her name is so well-known that you were looking forward to meeting him/her.

63

久闻大名

久闻 (jiǔ wén) means "hear long ago";
大名 (dà míng) "famous name".

久闻大名

jiǔ wén dà míng

I've heard many good things about you.

This expression is used as a courteous response when somebody introduces his/her name to you. It implies his/her name is so well-known that you were looking forward to meeting him/her.

别来无恙

别来 (**bié lái**) means "the time since we last saw each other"; 无恙 (**wú yàng**) "no illness".

别 来 无 恙

bié lái wú yàng

How have you been since we last met?

Used when you address a friend whom you haven't seen for some time. It implies both of you have a close relationship.

好自为之

好自 (**hǎo zì**) means "look out for yourself";
为之 (**wéi zhī**) "to do the job / thing".

hǎo   zì   wéi   zhī

Conduct yourself well and make the best of it.

This expression serves as advice, suggesting it would be wise not to take a second risk.

悬崖勒马

悬崖 (**xuán yá**) means "cliff/precipices";
勒马 (**lè mǎ**) "draw rein in one's horse".

悬崖勒马

xuán yá lè mǎ

Pull back before it is too late.

Used as advice or a warning to anyone who is facing danger and is not fully aware of the extent of the danger.

回头是岸

回头 (huí tóu) means "turn round";
是岸 (shì àn) "There is the shore".

回 头 是 岸

huí tóu shì àn

Repent and salvation is at hand.

Advice to someone who has committed a wrongdoing and needs to demonstrate regret for his action.

隔墙有耳

隔墙 (gé qiáng) means "the other side of the wall";
有耳 (yǒu ěr) "have ears".

隔 墙 有 耳

gé qiáng yǒu ěr

Walls have ears.

Used to warn people to beware of eavesdroppers.

三思后行

三思 (sān sī) means "think over and over";
后行 (hòu xíng) "to do/go later".

三思后行

sān sī hòu xíng

Look before you leap.

Used as advice to friends or colleagues.

早日康复

早日 (zǎo rì) means "soon";
康复 (kāng fù) "recover".

早日康复

zǎo rì kāng fù

Get well soon.

Used to encourage a sick friend.

好事多磨

好事 (hǎo shì) means "good things";
多磨 (duō mó) "much difficulty".

hǎo shì duō mó

Good things never come easily.

Used as a comfort to somone who has suffered setbacks in life.

81

塞翁失马

塞翁 (sài wēng) means "old men living at the frontier";
失马 (shī mǎ) "lost his horse".

塞翁失马

sài wēng shī mǎ

A loss may spell a gain.

Used to comfort someone who has met a misfortune. It comes from a tale in ancient China. An old man lost his mare and was sad, but a few days later the mare returned with a stallion. The expression implies that misfortune may turn out to be a blessing. It is also known as 塞翁失马 (sài wēng shī mǎ), 焉知非福 (yān zhī fēi fú)?

83

东山再起

东山 (dōng shān) literally means "East Mountain (A mountain east of Kuaiji, Zhejiang)". 东 implies the first place the sun rises; 再起 (zài qǐ) "rise again".

东 山 再 起

dōng shān zài qǐ

Stage a comeback.

Used when somebody has been removed from his post, severely criticized or punished.

来日方长

List of Winners

来日 (lái rì) means "days to come";
方长 (fāng cháng) "still long".

来 日 方 长

lái rì fāng cháng

There is ample time ahead of you/There will be other opportunities.

Used when somebody has failed and feels frustrated.

破财消灾

破财 (**pò cái**) means literally "loss of wealth";
消灾 (**xiāo zāi**) "misfortune vanished".

破财消灾

pò cái xiāo zāi

Such a loss may turn out to be a blessing.

Used when somebody has suffered from unexpected financial loss.

岁岁（碎碎）平安

岁岁 (suì suì) is a pun, its pronunciation carries either the
 meaning of "year in and year out" or " broken pieces";
平安 (píng ān) "peace".

岁 岁 平 安

suì suì píng ān

Peace every year.

Used when someone has broken something,
such as a cup or a bowl to comfort him.

节哀顺变

节哀 (jié āi) means "restrain one's grief";
顺变 (shùn biàn) "reconcile to the inevitable change".

节 哀 顺 变

jié āi shùn biàn

Don't be so sorrowful.

Used to offer condolences to those who have
just lost a family member or relative.

非常感谢

非常 (fēi cháng) means "very much";
感谢 (gǎn xiè) "be grateful".

非常感谢

fēi cháng gǎn xiè

Thank you very much.

Frequently used to express one's gratitude. It can be used on any occasion.

感激不尽

感激 (**gǎn jī**) means "to be grateful/feel indebted";
不尽 (**bú jìn**) "without end".

感激不尽

gǎn jī bú jìn

I am deeply indebted to you.

Used to express one's gratitude.

承蒙关照

承蒙 (chéng méng) is a courteous expression meaning deeply indebted; 关照 (guān zhào) "kind attention".

chéng méng guān zhào

Thank you for your care and consideration.

Used when you are especially well looked after.
(e.g. the special attention paid to you when you
go to work the first day.)

雪中送炭

雪中 (xuě zhōng) means "in the snowy weather";
送炭 (sòng tàn) "to send charcoal".

雪中送炭

xuě zhōng sòng tàn

Thank you for your timely assistance.

Used to describe somebody's timely help, especially when you are in need.

对不起

对不起 (**duì bu qǐ**) means "beg your pardon" or "I am sorry".

对不起

duì bu qǐ

I'm sorry/Excuse me.

The most frequently used expression to express one's apologies.

多多包涵

多多 (duō duō) means "much/ many";
包涵 (bāo hán) "excuse/forgive".

多多包涵

duō duō bāo hán

Please excuse (me for) what I have said/ done.

A courteous expression implying that you do not want to offend anyone.

哪里哪里

Double 哪里 (**nǎ li**) means "That's nothing".

nǎ li nǎ li

You are too kind. (Not at all).

Used as a modest response when you have been praised.

马马虎虎

马 (mǎ) literally means "horse"; 虎 (hǔ) "tiger".

马虎 When the two characters are combined, they mean
careless, casual. (also 马糊)

马马虎虎

mǎ mǎ hū hū

It is just so-so.

Used when something is only of so-so quality.

班门弄斧

Lu Ban

班门 (bān mén) means "in front of 鲁班(lǔ bān)"
   a real person who was an expert in carpentry;
弄斧 (nòng fǔ) means, "to wield the axe".

班门弄斧

bān mén nòng fǔ

Display one's inadequate skills in front of an expert.

A phrase to indicate humility in oneself or criticism of the skills of others.

抛砖引玉

抛砖 (pāo zhuān) means "to throw/cast bricks";
引玉 (yǐn yù) "to induce/attract jade".

抛砖引玉

pāo zhuān yǐn yù

May my crude remarks draw forth others by abler men.

Used when you want to induce someone to give you something valuable.

雕虫小技

雕虫 (**diāo chóng**) means "to carve insects";
小技 (**xiǎo jì**) "insignificant skill".

雕 虫 小 技

diāo chóng xiǎo jì

It is an insignificant skill/It is nothing accomplished to speak of.

Used as a courteous response when you are praised. (e.g. when someone is praising the dish you have cooked)

115

一路平安

一路 (yí lù) means "all the way/journey";
平安 (píng ān) "peaceful and safe".

一路平安

yí lù píng ān

Bon voyage.

Used for departures.

一路保重

一路 (**yí lù**) means "all the way/journey";
保重 (**bǎo zhòng**) "to take care".

一路保重

yí lù bǎo zhòng

Take care on your journey.

Used for departures.

一路顺风

一路 (yí lù) means "all the way/journey";
顺风 (shùn fēng) "have favorable wind".

一 路 顺 风

yí lù shùn fēng

Have a pleasant journey. Bon voyage.

Used for departures.

慢走

慢 (màn) literally means "slowly";
走 (zǒu) "to go".

慢 走

màn zǒu

Take care.

Used to say goodbye.

走好

走 (**zǒu**) means "to go";
好 (**hǎo**) "well".

zǒu　　hǎo

Take care.

Used to say goodbye.

胡说八道

胡说 (hú shuō) means "to talk nonsense";
八道 (bā dào) "groundless talk".

胡说八道

hú shuō bā dào

Nonsense!

Used to show the speaker's anger after hearing a groundless accusation.

讨厌

讨厌 (tǎo yàn) means "disgusting".

tǎo   yàn

What a nuisance!

Used to show one's resentment.

毛病

毛病 (máo bìng) literally means "disease".

máo bìng

You're crazy!

Used to show one's resentment.

忍无可忍

忍 (rěn) means "to bear";

无可忍 (wú kě rěn) "unable to bear".

忍无可忍

rěn wú kě rěn

This is too much to bear.

Used to express one's strong resentment.

白日做梦

白日 (bái rì) means "daytime";

做梦 (zuò mèng) "to dream".

白 日 做 梦

bái rì zuò mèng

Indulge in wishful thinking.

Used to express the wishfulness of one's thinking/thought. It implies that wishes will never come true.

合作愉快

合作 (**hé zuò**) means "to cooperate/cooperation";
愉快 (**yú kuài**) "happy and merry".

合作愉快

hé zuò yú kuài

May we have a fruitful cooperation.

Used when you start a business with a new partner.

道歉
Apology

自謙
Self-effacement

送別
Farewell

生氣不滿
Anger & Resentment

嘲諷
Irony

商務合作
Business Cooperation